SPEAK JAPANESE FOR BEGINNERS

A QUICK CRASH COURSE TO LEARN PHRASES, CULTURE AND THE LANGUAGE WITHOUT LEARNING KANJI AND KANA IF YOU'RE GOING TO JAPAN SOON!

YUKI HAYASHI

"If you talk to a man in a language he understands, that goes to his head. If you talk to him in his language, that goes to his heart." - Nelson Mandela

CONTENTS

Introduction   vii

1. Basics of Japanese Pronunciation   1
2. Essential Everyday Phrases   5
3. Numbers, Days, and Time   9
4. Food and Dining   16
5. Navigating Around   23
6. Japanese Culture and Etiquette   27
7. Fun and Entertainment   33
8. Handling Emergencies   37
9. Expanding Conversational Skills   40
10. Commonly Used Adjectives   43
11. Essential Phrase Cheat Sheet   48
12. Bonus: A Guide to the Main Cities in Japan   53
    Tokyo: The Capital and Beyond   55
    Kyoto: The Heart of Traditional Japan   57
    Osaka: The Kitchen of Japan   61
    Hiroshima: A City of Peace and Recovery   63
    Sapporo: The Northern Frontier   65
    Okinawa: The Tropical Paradise   67
    Nara: The Cradle of Japanese Tradition   71
13. Bonus: Itinerary   73
14. Conclusion   77
15. Arigatou gozaimasu   78

INTRODUCTION

Why Learn Japanese?

Japan is more than just a country of cherry blossoms, sushi, and anime. It is a nation with a rich history, deep-rooted traditions, and a unique perspective on the world. Learning Japanese allows one to:

- Dive deep into the world of Japanese arts, literature, and cinema.
- Improve business relations, given Japan's prominent role in the global economy.
- Foster personal growth by embracing a new way of thinking and understanding.

Plus, Japanese is spoken by over 125 million people. Engaging with them in their native language can be an incredibly rewarding experience.

Understanding the Structure of the Japanese Language

Japanese, unlike many Western languages, has a subject-object-verb (SOV) structure. For instance, in English, one would say "I drink coffee," but in Japanese, it would translate to "I coffee drink." This might seem unusual at first, but with consistent practice, this structure becomes intuitive.

Another notable feature is its system of honorifics, which reflects the societal emphasis on respect and hierarchy. Depending on whom you're addressing - a friend, a superior, or a stranger - your manner of speaking might change.

The Role of Kanji and Kana

Japanese writing involves three main scripts: Kanji, Hiragana, and Katakana (Kana). While this can be intimidating for beginners, it's essential to understand their role:

- Kanji: These are the characters borrowed from Chinese. Each Kanji has a meaning, and most have more than one pronunciation.
- Hiragana: This is the basic syllabary used for native Japanese words not covered by Kanji and for grammatical purposes.
- Katakana: Used primarily for foreign words and onomatopoeic expressions.

For the purpose of this book, while we acknowledge the importance of these scripts, we will primarily focus on speaking and understanding the language rather than reading and writing.

1. Basics of Japanese Pronunciation

Vowels and Consonants

Japanese pronunciation rests on a comparatively smaller set of sounds, making it more manageable for beginners. Here's a breakdown.

Vowels

Japanese has five vowels:

- a (pronounced as 'ah' like in 'car')
- e (pronounced as 'eh' like in 'bed')
- i (pronounced as 'ee' like in 'see')
- o (pronounced as 'oh' like in 'go')
- u (pronounced as 'oo' like in 'moon')

What's crucial to remember is that these sounds remain consistent, unlike in English where vowels can have multiple sounds. Japanese vowels can be either short or long, and distinguishing between them is essential for correct pronunciation.

Consonants

Many consonant sounds in Japanese are similar to their English counterparts, but there are a two main distinctions:

In the Japanese language, the 'r' sound is not the same as the English 'r' or the English 'l'. It's actually a sound that falls somewhere between the two. The tongue doesn't curl back as in the American English 'r', nor does it fully touch the roof of the mouth as in the English 'l'. Rather, it flaps against the alveolar ridge (the ridge just behind your upper front teeth) briefly, a bit like the 'tt' in the American pronunciation of "better."

The 'tsu' sound is a unique aspect of Japanese pronunciation that doesn't have a direct equivalent in English. This sound starts with a "t" and quickly transitions to an "s," both pronounced together very quickly as one syllable. English doesn't have any native words that begin with the 'ts' sound as a single syllable. However, you might hear it in some loanwords like "tsunami" or names like "Tchaikovsky."

Pitch Accent and Intonation

One of the characteristics that differentiates Japanese from many other languages is its pitch accent, which refers to the rise and fall of the voice when saying words.

- Flat Type: Some words have an even tone throughout.

- High-Low Type: The pitch rises on a specific syllable and drops sharply immediately after. For instance, the word for umbrella, "kasa," has a high pitch on "ka" and a low pitch on "sa."
- Low-High Type: Starts low and rises on a particular syllable, remaining high for the rest of the word.

Misplacing the pitch accent can change the meaning of a word. For instance, "hashi" can mean both "chopsticks" and "bridge" depending on the pitch.

Common Pronunciation Mistakes to Avoid

Consistent vowels: Unlike English, where a vowel can change its sound based on context (think of 'a' in "cat" vs. "car"), Japanese vowels always sound the same. Stick to the sounds mentioned above. Example: Consider the Japanese word "sakana" (fish) (saa-ka-na). The 'a' sound remains consistent in both syllables, sounding like the 'a' in "father" each time. It doesn't waver as it might in English words.

Not differentiating between short and long vowels: A short vowel is held for one beat, while a long vowel is held for two. For instance, 'o' in "Tokyo" is long, making it sound like "Towkyow." Example: Compare "obasan" (aunt) (oh-bah-san) with "obaasan" (grandmother) (oh-baah-san). The extended 'a' sound in "obaasan" makes all the difference in meaning. While both words have similar pronunciations, the duration of the 'a' vowel distinguishes one from the other.

Ignoring double consonants: In words like "sakki" (earlier) (sahk-khi), there's a brief pause before the second 'k.' This pause is essential and can change the word's meaning. Example: Contrast "kitte" (stamp) (kit-teh) with "kite" (come) (kit-eh). In "kitte," the double 't' necessitates a slight pause before pronouncing the 'te,' making the word sound distinct from "kite."

Misplaced pitch: As noted earlier, pitch accent is crucial. Words like "kami" (kah-me) can mean "paper," "god," or "hair" depending on the pitch. Example: With "kami": When referring to "god," the first syllable "ka" is stressed with a higher pitch, followed by a lower pitch on "mi." For "paper," both syllables have a flat or even pitch. For "hair," the first syllable "ka" has a lower pitch, rising to a higher pitch on "mi."

Overemphasizing the 'r': Remember, the Japanese 'r' is softer than the English one. It's not rolled, and it lies somewhere between the English 'l' and 'r' (like r/l). Example: Take the word "arigatou" (thank you) (ah-ri-gat-oh). In English, the 'r' in "river" is pronounced with a strong push from the tongue against the roof of the mouth. However, in "arigatou," the 'r' is lighter. The tongue taps quickly against the alveolar ridge, which is the bumpy area right behind the upper front teeth. This makes it sound closer to a blend between 'l' and 'r', almost like "ah-lee-gah-tou," but with a very soft 'r/l' sound.

2. Essential Everyday Phrases

Greetings and Introductions

The Japanese culture places great emphasis on greetings and politeness, which extend beyond mere words to encompass body language and tone.

Morning Greeting

Ohayou (oh-hah-yoh): "Good morning" in informal settings, like among friends or family.

Ohayou gozaimasu (oh-hah-yoh goh-zai-mahs): A more polite version of "Good morning," typically used in formal situations or with unfamiliar individuals.

Afternoon Greeting

Konnichiwa (kohn-nee-chee-wah): "Good afternoon" or just a general "Hello."

Evening Greeting

Konbanwa (kohn-bahn-wah): "Good evening."

Introducing Yourself

Watashi wa [Your Name] desu (wah-tah-shee wah [Your Name] deh-su): "I am [Your Name]."

Asking for Someone's Name

Onamae wa nan desu ka? (oh-nah-mah-eh wah nahn deh-su kah?): "What is your name?"

Expressing Gratitude

Expressing thanks is an integral part of Japanese interactions. The culture emphasizes showing gratitude not just for gifts or special deeds, but also in everyday contexts.

Thank You

Arigatou (ah-ree-gah-toh): An informal "Thank you."

Arigatou gozaimasu (ah-ree-gah-toh goh-zai-mahs): A more polite "Thank you," which is suitable for most scenarios.

Doumo arigatou gozaimasu (doh-moh ah-ree-gah-toh goh-zai-mahs): This is a very formal and courteous way of expressing

"Thank you very much" (to older people or your boss, the person you respect).

Response to Thanks

Dou itashimashite (doh ee-tah-shee-mahsh-teh): "You're welcome."

Asking for Help and Directions

If you find yourself in Japan, needing guidance or aid—be it at a shop, train station, or merely navigating around—knowing how to ask is crucial.

Asking for Help

Tasukete kudasai (tah-s-keh-teh koo-dah-sai): "Please help me." This phrase is more for situations that may be considered urgent.

Asking if Someone Speaks English

Eigo o hanasemasu ka? (ay-goh oh hah-nah-seh-mahs kah?): "Do you speak English?"

Asking for Directions

[Place] wa doko desu ka? ([Place] wah doh-koh deh-su kah?): "Where is [Place]?"

For instance, "Toire wa doko desu ka?" (toh-ee-reh wah doh-koh deh-su kah?) translates to "Where is the bathroom?"

Asking How to Get Somewhere

[Place] e douyatte ikimasu ka? ([Place] eh doh-yah-tteh ee-kee-mahs kah?): "How do I get to [Place]?"

Thanking Someone for Help

Tetsudatte kurete arigatou gozaimasu (teh-tsudah-teh koo-reh-teh ah-ree-gah-toh goh-zai-mahs): "Thank you for helping me."

3. Numbers, Days, and Time

Counting in Japanese

Counting is a fundamental skill in any language. In Japanese, the basics are pretty straightforward, though there are some unique number-related nuances to understand.

Basic Numbers

0: Rei (rei or zero)

1: Ichi (ee-chee)

2: Ni (nee)

3: San (sahn)

4: Shi or Yon (shee or yohn)

5: Go (goh)

6: Roku (roh-ku)

7: Shichi or Nana (shee-chee or nah-nah)

8: Hachi (hah-chee)

9: Kyuu or Ku (kyu or kew) kyū

10: Juu (joo)

20: Nijuu (nee-joo)

30: Sanjuu (sahn-joo)

40: Yonjuu (yohn-joo)

50: Gojuu (goh-joo)

60: Rokujuu (roh-ku-joo)

70: Nanajuu (nah-nah-joo)

80: Hachijuu (hah-chee-joo)

90: Kyuujuu (kyu-joo)

Note: For numbers beyond ten, you'd typically combine the tens and units. For instance, 11 would be "Juu-ichi" (10 + 1), 12 would be "Juu-ni" (10 + 2), and so on.

100: Hyaku (hee-yah-ku)

Hyaku means one hundred in Japanese. However, as you count upwards in hundreds, some numbers have irregular pronunciations:

200: Nihyaku (nee-hyah-koo) 'oo' as in 'cooing'

300: Sanbyaku (sahn-byah-koo)

400: Yonhyaku (yohn-hyah-koo)

500: Gohyaku (goh-hyah-koo)

600: Roppyaku (roh-ppyah-koo)

700: Nanahyaku (nah-nah-hyah-koo)

800: Happyaku (hah-ppyah-koo)

900: Kyuuhyaku (kyoo-hyah-koo)

You'll notice that while 100 is straightforward, numbers like 300 and 600 introduce a slight sound change (the added "b" and "pp" sounds). These sound changes are due to phonetic shifts that make the words easier to pronounce in the flow of speech.

1,000: Sen (sehn) or Chi (chee) in some compounds

Sen stands for one thousand. Similar to hundreds, there are some deviations when counting by thousands:

1,000: Sen (sehn)

2,000: Nisen (nee-sehn) - Here, you'll notice the standard 'Ni' for two.

3,000: Sanzen (sahn-zen) - The "zen" here is a phonetic shift from "sen."

4,000: Yonsen (yohn-sehn)

5,000: Gosen (goh-sehn)

6,000: Rokusen (roh-koo-sehn)

7,000: Nanasen (nah-nah-sehn)

8,000: Hassen (hahs-sehn)

9,000: Kyuusen (kyoo-sehn)

For values over 10,000, the Japanese use a new term, 'mahn'. 10,000 would be Ichi-man (ee-chee-mahn), and the pattern continues, combining units, tens, hundreds, thousands with 'mahn' for larger numbers.

Grasping these larger numbers allows for more intricate conversations about prices, quantities, and statistics. It's not uncommon for beginners to find these slightly challenging initially, but continuous exposure and practice will make them second nature. It's also worth noting that understanding these number systems is essential for tasks such as currency conversion, especially when dealing with yen, which frequently deals in the thousands and ten-thousands.

Days of the Week

Days of the week in Japanese are based on elements, which is a unique feature compared to many other languages.

Monday: Getsuyoubi (geht-soo-yoh-bee) - "Moon Day"

Tuesday: Kayoubi (kah-yoh-bee) - "Fire Day"

Wednesday: Suiyoubi (soo-ee-yoh-bee) - "Water Day"

Thursday: Mokuyoubi (moh-koo-yoh-bee) - "Wood Day"

Friday: Kinyoubi (keen-yoh-bee) - "Gold/Metal Day"

Saturday: Doyoubi (doh-yoh-bee) - "Earth Day"

Sunday: Nichiyoubi (nee-chee-yoh-bee) - "Sun Day"

Discussing Time and Dates

Conveying time and dates in Japanese requires an understanding of both numbers and the terms used to denote time periods.

. . .

Hours

When expressing time in Japanese, you use the basic number system for hours followed by "ji":

1 o'clock: Ichi-ji (ee-chee-jee)

2 o'clock: Ni-ji (nee-jee)

3 o'clock: San-ji (sahn-jee)

4 o'clock: Yon-ji (yo-jee)

5 o'clock: Go-ji (goh-jee)

6 o'clock: Roku-ji (roh-koo-jee)

7 o'clock: Shichi-ji (shee-chee-jee)

8 o'clock: Hachi-ji (hah-chee-jee)

9 o'clock: Ku-ji (koo-jee)

10 o'clock: Juu-ji (joo-jee)

11 o'clock: Juu-ichi-ji (joo-ee-chee-jee)

12 o'clock: Juu-ni-ji (joo-nee-jee)

For times like half-past, you'd use the term "han".

3:30 would be San-ji han (sahn-jee hahn).

7:30, conversely, is Shichi-ji han (shee-chee-jee hahn).

Minutes

When you express minutes, the pattern is fairly regular. Here are additional examples:

5 minutes: Go-fun (goh-foon)

10 minutes: Juu-fun (joo-foon)

15 minutes: Juu-go-fun (joo-goh-foon)

20 minutes: Nijuu-fun (nee-joo-foon)

25 minutes: Nijuu-go-fun (nee-joo-goh-foon)

30 minutes: Sanjuu-fun (sahn-joo-foon)

35 minutes: Sanjuu-go-fun (sahn-joo-goh-foon)

40 minutes: Yonjuu-fun (yohn-joo-foon)

45 minutes: Yonjuu-go-fun (yohn-joo-goh-foon)

50 minutes: Gojuu-fun (goh-joo-foon)

55 minutes: Gojuu-go-fun (goh-joo-goh-foon)

These patterns should help you construct any time you'd like to express in Japanese. Remember that, in conversations, practice and repetition will make these terms feel more natural over time.

Days, Months, Years

Today: Kyou (kyoh)

Tomorrow: Ashita (ah-sh-tah)

Yesterday: Kinou (kee-noh)

Day: Hi (hee)

Month: Tsuki (tsoo-kee)

Year: Toshi (toh-shee)

In Japan, the date format is typically Year-Month-Day. When you want to say a specific date like the 5th of April 2023, you would say it as follows:

"Nisen nijuu-san nen shi-gatsu itsuka."

- "Nisen nijuu-san nen" means "the year 2023" (literally "two thousand twenty-three year").
- "Shi-gatsu" means "April" (fourth month).
- "Itsuka" means "the fifth day."

So, "Nisen nijuu-san nen shi-gatsu itsuka" translates to "The 5th of April 2023" in English.

Understanding numbers, days, and time in Japanese is vital not only for scheduling and logistics but also for daily life scenarios like shopping, making appointments, or catching public transport. As with all language learning, practice makes perfect, so repeat these terms regularly to internalize them.

4. Food and Dining

Food is an integral part of Japanese culture, known worldwide for its deliciousness, precision, and presentation. This chapter will guide you through essential phrases and knowledge needed for dining out in Japan.

Ordering in Restaurants

When you first enter a restaurant, it's customary to be greeted with "Irasshaimase!" (Eera-shai-maas-eh) which means "Welcome!"

Asking for a Table

For two: "Futari desu." (Foo-tah-ree dess) – This means "For two."

If you have a reservation: "Yoyaku shiteimasu. [Your Name] desu." (Yoh-yah-koo shee-teh-ee-mahs. [Your Name] dess) – This translates to "I have a reservation. I am [Your Name]."

Ordering Food and Drinks

"Kore o kudasai." (Koh-reh oh koo-dah-sigh) – "I'll have this." Often, you can just point to the menu item.

"Omizu kudasai." (Oh-mee-zoo koo-dah-sigh) – "Water, please."

Special Requests

"Onegaishimasu" (Oh-neh-guy-shee-mahs) – This is a polite way to say "please" when making a request.

"Dekireba" (Deh-kee-reh-bah) – "If possible..."

Paying the Bill

"Okaikei onegaishimasu." (Oh-kigh-kay oh-neh-guy-shee-mahs) – "Check, please."

"Genkin de haraimasu." (Gen-keen deh hah-rye-mahs) – "I'll pay in cash." (It's super important to mention that in Japan, you don't need to leave a tip, as this is considered rude or that the food wasn't good enough).

Popular Japanese Dishes

Japanese cuisine offers a wide variety of dishes. Here are some of the most popular ones you might encounter:

Sushi – Raw fish on vinegar-seasoned rice. Varieties include Nigiri (fish on rice) and Maki (rolled sushi).

Ramen – A noodle soup with various toppings such as pork, green onions, and sometimes a boiled egg.

Tempura – Deep-fried vegetables and seafood.

Sashimi – Sliced raw fish.

Yakitori – Grilled chicken skewers.

Udon – Thick wheat noodles often served in a soup.

Okonomiyaki – A savory pancake containing a variety of ingredients.

Dietary Restrictions and Preferences

It's essential to communicate any dietary restrictions or preferences when dining out. Here are some phrases to help:

Vegetarian

"Watashi wa bejitarian desu." (Wah-tah-shee wah beh-jee-tah-ree-ahn dess) – "I am a vegetarian."

Vegan

"Watashi wa vegan desu." (Wah-tah-shee wah vee-gan dess) – "I am a vegan."

Allergies

"Watashi wa [allergen] arerugii ga arimasu." (Wah-tah-shee wah [allergen] ah-leh-roo-gee gah ah-ree-mahs) – "I am allergic to [allergen]."

No Pork

"Buta niku nashi de onegaishimasu." (Boo-tah nee-koo nah-shee deh oh-neh-guy-shee-mahs) – "Without pork, please."

No Alcohol

"Aruko-ru nashi de onegaishimasu." (Ah-roo-koh-roo nah-shee deh oh-neh-guy-shee-mahs) – "Without alcohol, please."

Understanding these phrases and dishes will make your dining experience in Japan smoother and more enjoyable. Always remember to say "Arigatou gozaimasita" (Ah-ree-gah-toh goh-zai-mahs-see-ta) – "Thank you very much (for everything)!" – when leaving, to show appreciation for the service.

Other things to know: The Unwritten Rules of Japanese Dining Experiences

Izakaya otoshi

"Izakaya otoshi" refers to a small appetizer served at izakayas in Japan. An izakaya is a type of Japanese drinking establishment that serves food as well. When you sit down at an izakaya, you'll often be given an otoshi before you even order. This appetizer is not free; the cost is automatically added to your bill as a seating charge. The practice might be surprising to those unfamiliar with it, but it is customary in Japan.

The type of otoshi you receive can vary widely depending on the establishment and what they have available. It could be anything from a small dish of edamame (young soybeans) to a more elaborate seasonal delicacy. The idea is to provide a little something to snack on while you peruse the menu and decide on your drinks and food orders.

In some ways, you can think of an otoshi as similar to bread served at some Western restaurants, although in Western settings the bread is often complimentary. The otoshi serves as a sort of informal kick-off to your meal and is an integral part of the izakaya experience.

Nomihodai

"Nomihodai" is a Japanese term that translates to "all-you-can-drink." It's a promotion commonly offered at izakayas, bars, and restaurants in Japan, where customers can enjoy unlimited alcoholic beverages for a set period (usually ranging from 90 minutes to 2 hours) and a fixed price. This deal is popular among groups of friends and coworkers looking to have a good time without worrying too much about the cost.

There are often rules and restrictions to keep in mind:

- Time Limit: As mentioned, nomihodai usually has a time limit. Once the time is up, the all-you-can-drink offer expires, and you'll need to pay regular price for additional drinks.
- Limited Menu: The drinks available for nomihodai are typically limited to a select menu, which may include beer, wine, various cocktails, and non-alcoholic options. Top-shelf or premium drinks are generally not included.
- Everyone Participates: Usually, if one person in a group opts for nomihodai, everyone else at the table must also participate in the deal.
- No Wastage: Some establishments have rules against wasting drinks, meaning you can't order a new one until you've finished the previous one.

- Order Pace: Some places may have restrictions on how quickly you can order new drinks. You might be required to finish your current drink before ordering another.
- Food Orders: Some establishments require you to order food along with the nomihodai option, while others might offer a separate "tabehodai" (all-you-can-eat) deal that can be combined with nomihodai.

It's essential to be respectful of the establishment's rules and mindful of your alcohol consumption when taking advantage of a nomihodai offer. Overindulgence not only risks your health but is also frowned upon socially in Japan.

The cost of a nomihodai promotion in Japan can vary widely depending on the establishment, location, and the quality of beverages included. You could generally expect to pay around 1,500 to 3,000 Japanese yen ($15 to $30 USD) for a ninety minute to two hour all-you-can-drink deal.

Tabehoudai

"Tabehoudai" (sometimes spelled "tabehodai") is a Japanese term that translates to "all-you-can-eat." This is a promotion offered by some restaurants in Japan where diners can enjoy unlimited servings of food for a set price and within a specific time frame, usually ranging from 90 minutes to 2 hours. The concept is similar to "nomihodai," which is an all-you-can-drink offer.

The type of cuisine offered in a tabehoudai setting can vary widely. You might find all-you-can-eat offers for specific types of food like sushi, yakiniku (grilled meat), shabu-shabu (Japanese hotpot), or even desserts. Some establishments might offer a broad range of foods as part of a buffet.

As with nomihodai, there are usually rules and conditions that diners must follow:

- Time Limit: The offer is valid for a specific duration. Once the time is up, you can't order more food without paying extra.
- Waste Policy: Most restaurants discourage wasting food. You may be required to finish your current plate before ordering more, and some places may charge extra if you leave food uneaten.
- Everyone Participates: In many cases, if one person at the table opts for the tabehoudai option, everyone else must also participate.
- Limited Menu: The all-you-can-eat offer might be limited to a specific menu or range of items.
- Ordering Restrictions: Some establishments have an ordering system where you must place new orders through a waiter, and you might need to finish your current dish before ordering the next.
- Combination with Nomihodai: Some places offer both tabehoudai and nomihodai, and you might be able to combine both offers for a set price.

Tabehoudai can be an excellent way to enjoy a wide variety of dishes at a reasonable price, but it's important to be mindful of the rules and respectful of the restaurant's policies. Overeating or wasting food is generally considered disrespectful, so it's best to order only as much as you can comfortably eat.

The cost of a tabehoudai is similar to a nomihodai, around 1,500 to 3,000 Japanese yen ($15 to $30 USD) for a ninety minute to two hour all-you-can-eat experience.

5. Navigating Around

Japan's vast urban landscapes and historic towns make navigating an exciting but sometimes challenging experience, especially if you're not familiar with the language. Equip yourself with these essential phrases and knowledge to get around with ease.

Transportation Phrases

Navigating Japan's efficient transportation system is much simpler when you know some fundamental phrases:

Buying a Ticket

"Kippu o kudasai." (Kee-poo oh koo-dah-sigh) - "A ticket, please."

"Kippu o nimai kudasai." (Kee-poo oh nee-migh koo-dah-sigh) - "Two tickets, please."

Asking for the Right Train or Bus

"Tokyo eki made no densha wa dore desu ka?" (Toh-kyoh eh-kee mah-deh no den-shah wah doh-reh dess kah?) - "Which train goes to Tokyo station?"

Inquiring About Departure Time

"Kono densha wa nanji ni shuppatsu shimasu ka?" (Koh-noh den-shah wah nahn-jee nee shoo-pah-tsoo shee-mahs kah?) - "What time does this train depart?"

Asking for and Giving Directions

In Japan, it's common for streets not to have names, making directions a bit challenging. Instead of traditional street names and numbers, addresses are typically based on a system of numbered blocks and districts. Cities and towns are divided into smaller sections or neighborhoods, and each of these sections is assigned a number. Buildings within these sections are then numbered sequentially based on when they were constructed.

For example, an address in Japan might look something like this:

1-2-3 Shibuya, Tokyo

- The "1" represents the block or district within Shibuya.
- The "2" represents a sub-block or section within that district.
- The "3" represents the specific building or house number within that sub-block.

This system relies heavily on landmarks, major streets, and local knowledge to navigate effectively, as there are often no street names to guide you. Consequently, when asking for directions or giving directions in Japan, it's common to reference well-known landmarks, public transportation stations, or businesses to help people find their way.

However, people are generally very helpful so don't be afraid to ask.

Getting Clarity

"Motto yukkuri onegaishimasu." (Moh-toh yoo-koo-ree oh-neh-guy-shee-mahs) - "Please speak more slowly."

Some Common Directional Phrases

"Masugu" (Mah-soo-gu) - "Straight."

"Migi" (Mee-gee) - "Right."

"Hidari" (Hee-dah-ree) - "Left."

"Tonari" (Toh-nah-ree) - "Next to."

"Ushiro" (Oo-shee-ro) - "Behind."

Important Locations and Landmarks

It's crucial to familiarize yourself with some standard landmarks and locations when navigating a new city. Here are some important terms:

Train/Subway Stations: "Eki" (Eh-kee)

Bus Stops: "Basu tei" (Bah-soo teh-ee)

Tourist Information: "Kankou annaijo" (Kahn-koh ahn-nigh-joh)

Hospitals: "Byouin" (Byoh-een)

Police Station: "Kouban" (Koh-bahn)

Temple: "Tera" (Teh-rah)

Shrine: "Jinja" (Jeen-jah)

Recognizing these words, combined with the directional phrases, will assist in making your navigation around Japan much more manageable. Remember always to remain polite and express gratitude ("Arigatou gozaimasu") when someone assists you.

6. Japanese Culture and Etiquette

Japanese culture is deeply rooted in tradition, and their customs reflect a unique blend of the old and the new. For visitors, understanding these customs can enhance the overall experience in Japan, fostering respectful interactions and deeper connections.

Social Norms and Behaviors

Bowing: "Ojigi" (oh-jee-gee)

One of the most recognized gestures, bowing, signifies respect, gratitude, and humility. The deeper the bow, the more respect it indicates.

While bowing is a common and respectful gesture in Japanese culture, foreigners visiting Japan are not expected to bow in the same formal and traditional manner as native Japanese people. Japanese people understand that visitors may not be familiar with all aspects of their culture and customs, including bowing.

However, it is appreciated when foreigners make an effort to show respect by acknowledging and reciprocating bows when they are offered. You don't need to perform deep bows, but a slight nod of the head or a small, respectful bow can be a polite way to respond when someone bows to you. It's a sign of cultural awareness and respect for the local customs.

Greetings

Morning: "Ohayou gozaimasu" (oh-hah-yoh goh-zai-mahs) - "Good morning."

Afternoon/Evening: "Konbanwa" (kohn-bahn-wah) - "Good evening."

General: "Konnichiwa" (kohn-nee-chee-wah) - "Hello."

Using Both Hands

When giving or receiving something (like money or a card), use both hands. It shows respect for the item and the person.

Speaking Softly

Japanese culture values discretion and politeness. Raising one's voice or being overtly expressive in public spaces can be viewed as impolite.

Public Behavior

Avoid talking loudly or using phones on public transportation. Eating while walking is generally frowned upon in most places, though there are exceptions like festivals.

Gift Giving and Receiving

Omiyage (oh-mee-yah-geh) - Souvenir

When traveling, it's a custom to buy local souvenirs (usually snacks) to share with friends, family, and coworkers upon returning.

Presentation

The way a gift is wrapped is as essential as the gift itself. It symbolizes care and respect.

Receiving Gifts

When receiving a gift, it's polite to decline initially lightly. If the giver insists, accept it with both hands and express gratitude. Open the gift later unless the giver encourages you to do so immediately.

Seasonal Gifting

There are two primary gifting seasons in Japan: summer (Ochugen) and year-end (Oseibo). During these times, people give appreciation gifts to those who have helped them. This is usually more common with older generations.

Visiting a Japanese Home

Shoes Off

Always remove your shoes before entering someone's home. You may be provided with indoor slippers.

Bringing a Gift

It's customary to bring a small gift when visiting someone's home as a gesture of appreciation. Here are some examples of gifts that are suitable for such occasions:

- **Omiyage**: These are regional souvenirs or specialty items from your hometown or a place you've recently visited. They can be snacks, sweets, or local crafts.
- **Sweets**: High-quality Japanese sweets, such as wagashi (traditional Japanese confections), are often appreciated. You can also consider bringing chocolates or other candies.
- **Tea**: Green tea, especially matcha (powdered green tea), is a popular and thoughtful gift. You can opt for loose leaf tea or tea bags.
- **Fruit**: High-quality, seasonal fruit like Japanese persimmons or melons is considered a luxurious gift.
- **Alcohol**: A bottle of sake or a fine Japanese whisky can be a good choice if you know the host enjoys alcoholic beverages.
- **Flowers**: A bouquet of fresh flowers, particularly in odd numbers, is a classic and elegant gift. However, avoid bringing white flowers, which are associated with funerals in Japan.

- **Tableware**: Traditional Japanese tableware, like sake cups or chopstick sets, can be a thoughtful and lasting gift.
- **Decorative Items**: Small decorative items or home decor, such as a vase or a decorative lantern, can be a nice addition to someone's home.
- **Books or Stationery**: If your host enjoys reading, a book or a stylish notebook can be a thoughtful present.

Dining Etiquette

Wait for the host to signal the start of the meal. It's polite to say "Itadakimasu" (ee-tah-dah-kee-mahs) - "I humbly receive" before eating and "Gochisousama" (goh-chee-soh-sah-mah) after finishing which is a way to show appreciation and gratitude to the host or the person who prepared the meal. It can be translated as "thank you for the meal" or "that was delicious."

Bathroom Etiquette

Most homes will have separate bathroom slippers. Remember to change back into the indoor slippers after using the bathroom and not to walk around the house in bathroom slippers.

Saying Goodbye

After a visit, it's common for the host to accompany the guest to the door or even outside. The guest should give a final bow and express gratitude for the hospitality.

· · ·

By understanding and respecting these cultural norms and practices, visitors can foster more profound and more meaningful connections during their time in Japan. It's always appreciated when foreigners make an effort to acknowledge local customs.

7. Fun and Entertainment

Japanese entertainment spans a rich tapestry of ancient traditions and contemporary passions. From vibrant festivals that light up the skies to modern sports that capture the nation's heart, the Japanese know how to celebrate and unwind.

Popular Festivals and Celebrations

Hanami (Cherry Blossom Viewing):

When: Spring (March, April, and sometimes early May)

Celebrate the fleeting beauty of cherry blossoms. Parks get crowded with people enjoying picnics under the blooming trees.

Tanabata (Star Festival):

When: July 7

Commemorates the story of two star-crossed lovers allowed to meet just once a year. People write wishes on colorful strips of paper and hang them on bamboo branches.

Gion Matsuri (Gion Festival):

When: July

One of Japan's most famous festivals, it involves processions of large floats in Kyoto, accompanied by traditional music.

Obon (Festival of the Dead):

When: August

A Buddhist event where families honor deceased ancestors. Lanterns are lit and dances called Bon Odori are performed.

Nebuta Matsuri (Summer Festival):

When: August

Held in Aomori, this festival showcases massive, brightly colored lantern floats paraded through the streets.

Sports and Recreational Activities

Sumo Wrestling

Japan's national sport, Sumo, has a history spanning many centuries and is a must-watch if you're in Tokyo during one of its grand tournaments.

Baseball

Highly popular in Japan, attending a baseball game can be an electrifying experience, with local fans displaying deep passion and unique cheering styles.

Martial Arts

From Judo to Karate to Kendo, martial arts form an integral part of Japanese culture. Many dojos offer trial sessions for visitors.

Onsen

Relaxing in a natural hot spring is a beloved Japanese pastime. These are found throughout the country and offer therapeutic relaxation.

Karaoke

An essential Japanese recreational activity, where friends and family sing along to popular tunes in private booths.

Engaging in Small Talk

Weather

A safe topic, similar to many cultures. "Ii tenki desu ne?" (ee ten-kee des ne) translates to "Nice weather, isn't it?"

Hobbies

Asking about someone's hobbies can open up delightful conversations. "Shumi wa nan desu ka?" (shoo-mee wa nan des ka) means "What are your hobbies?"

Travel

Discussing recent or future travel plans can be engaging. "Saikin doko ka ni ryokou shimashita ka?" (sigh-keen doko ka ni ryo-koh shee-mash-ta ka) translates to "Have you traveled anywhere recently?"

Movies and Music

Pop culture always serves as a good icebreaker. "Saikin no suki na eiga wa nan desu ka?" (sigh-keen no soo-kee na ay-ga wa nan des ka) means "What's your recent favorite movie?"

Food

Discussing local cuisines, restaurants, or dishes can be both informative and delightful. "Nihon no tabemono wa suki desu ka?" (nee-hon no tah-beh-mo-no wa soo-kee des ka) translates to "Do you like Japanese food?"

By engaging in these activities and conversations, one can delve deeper into Japanese culture, making connections that last beyond the duration of a trip. Remember, it's not just about the activities but also about the shared moments and understanding that they foster.

8. Handling Emergencies

Navigating unexpected emergencies in a foreign land can be a daunting experience. However, knowing some key phrases and understanding the protocols can make all the difference. This chapter aims to equip you with essential knowledge and phrases to manage emergencies in Japan.

Health and Safety Phrases

I need a doctor: "Isha ni ai tai desu" (ee-shah nee aye tai des).

Call an ambulance: "Kyūkyūsha o yonde kudasai" (kyoo-kyoo-shah oh yohn-deh koo-dah-sai).

I'm not feeling well: "Kibun ga warui desu" (kee-boon gah wah-roo-ee des).

I'm allergic to...: "... no arerugī ga arimasu" (... no ah-le-roo-gee gah ah-ree-mahs). Insert the name of the allergen where the ellipsis is.

It's an emergency: "Kinkyūjitaidesu" (kin-kyoo-jee-tai des).

Medicine: "Kusuri" (koo-soo-ree).

Hospital: "Byōin" (byoh-een).

Lost and Found

I've lost my...: "... o nakushimashita" (... oh nah-koo-shee-mah-shi-tah). Fill in the blank with the item you've lost, e.g., "passport" would be "pasupōto."

Where is the lost and found?: "Otoshitabasho wa doko desu ka?" (Oh-toh-shee-ta-ba-sho wah doh-koh des ka).

I've found a...: "... o mitsukemashita" (... oh mit-soo-keh-mah-shi-tah). Replace the ellipsis with the name of the item you found.

Is this yours?: "Kore wa anata no desu ka?" (koh-reh wah ah-nah-tah no des ka).

Seeking Assistance

Help: "Tasukete" (tah-soo-keh-teh).

Police: "Keisatsu" (kay-saht-su).

Can you help me?: "Tetsudatte moraemasu ka?" (teht-su-daht-teh moh-ra-eh-mahs ka).

I need a translator: "Honyaku-sha ga hitsuyō desu" (hohn-yah-koo-shah gah hee-tsuyoh des).

Is there anyone who speaks English?: "Eigo o hanaseru hito wa imasu ka?" (ay-goh oh hah-nah-seh-roo hee-toh wah ee-mahs ka).

Remember, the Japanese are generally helpful and will often go out of their way to assist you, even if they don't speak your language fluently. In major cities, you can also find information centers, train stations, and tourist spots where English-speaking staff are available. When dealing with emergencies, it's also essential to remain calm and approach someone trustworthy for help, like the police (known as "Koban" in Japan) or staff at local establishments.

9. Expanding Conversational Skills

Enhancing your proficiency in Japanese goes beyond just knowing the words; it's about constructing sentences, expressing yourself, and engaging in meaningful dialogue. This chapter is designed to help you elevate your conversational prowess in Japanese.

Forming Simple Sentences

Japanese sentence structure can be unique. A fundamental distinction is that, in Japanese, the verb typically comes at the end of the sentence. Let's begin with some basic patterns:

Subject-Object-Verb (SOV) structure: Unlike English, which uses a Subject-Verb-Object structure, Japanese often employs SOV.

English: I (subject) eat (verb) an apple (object).

Japanese: Watashi wa ringo o tabemasu (I an apple eat). (wah-tah-shee wah reen-goh oh tah-beh-mas).

Describing things: Use the "desu" pattern.

This is a book: Kore wa hon desu (koreh-wa-hon-des)

Arisa is a teacher: Arisa san wa sensei desu (Ah-ree-sah sahn wah sehn-sei deh-su).

Talking about likes: Use the "suki" pattern.

I like cats: Neko ga suki desu (neh-koh gah soo-kee deh-su).

Asking Questions and Making Requests

Basic Questions: Often, just adding "ka" at the end of a sentence turns it into a question.

It's a book: Kore wa hon desu (Koh-reh wah hohn deh-su)

Is it a book?: Kore wa hon desu ka? (Koh-reh wah hohn deh-su kah?)

Asking "What": "Nani" or "Nan" is used for "what."

What is this?: Kore wa nan desu ka? (Koh-reh wah nahn deh-su kah?)

Making Requests: The verb form "te-kudasai" is often used to make polite requests.

Please wait: Matte kudasai (mah-tteh koo-dah-sigh)

Please eat: Tabete kudasai (tah-beh-teh koo-dah-sigh)

Expressing Emotions and Feelings

I'm happy: Ureshii desu (oo-re-shee-ee des).

I'm sad: Kanashii desu (kah-nah-shee-ee des).

I'm angry: Okotteimasu (oh-koh-tteh-ee-mahs).

I'm tired: Tsukareteimasu (tsu-kah-reh-teh-ee-mahs).

I'm surprised: Odoroiteimasu (oh-doh-roh-ee-teh-ee-mahs).

Also, remember the power of context. In many conversational settings, the Japanese drop the subject of a sentence when it's clear who or what they're talking about. So, the sentence "Watashi wa ureshii desu" (I'm happy) can be shortened to just "Ureshii desu" in the right context.

By combining these sentence structures, questions, and expressions, you can form a wide array of sentences to converse effectively in various situations. As always, practice is key. Engage in dialogues, listen to native speakers, and immerse yourself in various forms of Japanese media to hone these skills.

10. Commonly Used Adjectives

Big

Okii (oh-kee-ee). Examples of usage:

Big house: Okii ie (oh-kee-ee ee-eh)

Big dog: Okii inu (oh-kee-ee ee-noo)

Small

Chisai (chee-sigh). Examples of usage:

Small flower: Chisai hana (chee-sigh hah-nah)

Small town: Chisai machi (chee-sigh mah-chee)

Beautiful

Kirei (kee-ray). Examples of usage:

Beautiful person: Kirei na hito (kee-ray nah hee-toh)

Beautiful night sky: Kirei na yozora (kee-ray nah yoh-zoh-rah)

Ugly

Minikui (mee-nee-koo-ee). Examples of usage:

Ugly rat: Minikui nezumi (mee-nee-koo-ee neh-zoo-mee)

Ugly clock: Minikui tokei (mee-nee-koo-ee toh-keh-ee)

Hot

Atsui (aht-soo-ee). Examples of usage:

Hot coffee: Atsui kōhī (aht-soo-ee koh-hee)

Hot day: Atsui hi (aht-soo-ee hee)

Cold

Samui (sah-moo-ee). Examples of usage:

Cold night: Samui yoru (sah-moo-ee yoh-roo)

Cold day: Samui hi (sah-moo-ee hee)

Fast

Hayai (hah-yah-ee). Examples of usage:

Fast car: Hayai kuruma (hah-yah-ee koo-roo-mah)

Fast train: Hayai densha (hah-yah-ee dehn-shah)

Slow

Osoi (oh-soh-ee). Examples of usage:

Slow turtle: Osoi kame (oh-soh-ee kah-meh)

Slow bird: Osoi tori (oh-soh-ee toh-ree)

Commonly Used Verbs

To eat

Tabemasu (tah-beh-mas). Examples of usage:

To eat a meal: Gohan o tabemasu (goh-hahn oh tah-beh-mas)

To eat fish: Sakana o tabemasu (sah-kah-nah oh tah-beh-mas)

To go

Ikimasu (ee-kee-mas). Examples of usage:

To go to see a movie: Eiga o mini ikimasu (eh-ee-gah oh mee-nee ee-kee-mas)

To go to Japan: Nihon e ikimasu (nee-hohn eh ee-kee-mas)

To see/watch

Mimasu (mee-mas). Examples of usage:

To watch television: Terebi o mimasu (teh-reh-bee oh mee-mas)

To look at the stars: Hoshi o mimasu (hoh-shee oh mee-mas)

To drink

Nomimasu (noh-mee-mas). Examples of usage:

To drink water: Mizu o nomimasu (mee-zoo oh noh-mee-mas)

To drink wine: Wain o nomimasu (wah-een oh noh-mee-mas)

To listen

Kikimasu (kee-kee-mas). Examples of usage:

To listen to music: Ongaku o kikimasu (ohn-gah-koo oh kee-kee-mas)

To listen to the radio: Radio o kikimasu (rah-dee-oh oh kee-kee-mas)

To speak/talk

Hanashimasu (hah-nah-shee-mas). Examples of usage:

To speak English: Eigo o hanashimasu (eh-ee-goh oh hah-nah-shee-mas)

To talk with a friend: Tomodachi to hanashimasu (toh-moh-dah-chee toh hah-nah-shee-mas)

To come

Kimasu (kee-mas). Examples of usage:

To come to my house: Uchi e kimasu (oo-chee eh kee-mas)

To come to Tokyo: Tokyo e kimasu (toh-kyoh eh kee-mas)

To buy

Kaimasu (kai-mas). Examples of usage:

To buy a book: Hon o kaimasu (hohn oh kai-mas)

To buy shoes: Kutsu o kaimasu (koo-tsoo oh kai-mas)

These are fundamental terms in the Japanese language. While they provide a foundational understanding, it's essential to continue expanding one's vocabulary and practice to achieve fluency.

11. Essential Phrase Cheat Sheet

General Phrases

Hello: Konnichiwa (koh-nee-chee-wah)

Goodbye: Sayonara (sigh-yoh-nah-rah)

Please: Onegaishimasu (oh-neh-gai-shee-mahs)

Thank you: Arigatou (ah-ree-gah-toh)

Yes: Hai (hah-ee)

No: Iie (ee-eh)

Getting Around

Where is...?: ... wa doko desu ka? (wah doh-koh dess kah?)

Train station: Eki (eh-kee)

Bus stop: Basu tei (bah-sew tay)

Taxi: Takushī (tah-koo-shee)

Eating and Drinking

I'm hungry: Onaka ga sukimashita (oh-nah-kah gah su-kee-mah-shee-tah)

Water: Mizu (mee-zoo)

Beer: Bīru (bee-roo)

Check, please: Okaikei onegaishimasu (oh-kah-ee-kay oh-neh-gai-shee-mahs)

Shopping

How much is this?: Kore wa ikura desu ka? (koh-ray wah ee-koo-rah dess kah?)

Expensive: Takai (tah-kigh)

Cheap: Yasui (yah-soo-ee)

Emergency

Help!: Tasukete! (tah-soo-keh-teh)

I'm lost: Mayoimashita (mah-yoh-ee-mah-shee-tah)

Hospital: Byōin (byoh-een)

Business and Formal

Nice to meet you: Hajimemashite (hah-jee-meh-mah-shee-teh)

My name is...: Watashi no namae wa...desu (wah-tah-shee no nah-mah-eh wah...dess)

I have a reservation: Yoyaku ga arimasu (yoh-yah-koo gah ah-ree-mah-soo)

Others

Sorry: Gomen nasai (goh-men nah-sigh)

I don't understand: Wakarimasen (wah-kah-ree-mah-sehn)

Do you speak English?: Eigo o hanasemasu ka? (ay-goh oh hah-nah-seh-mahs kah?)

Practice Dialogues

Dialogue 1: Greeting and Introduction

Person A: Hello. (konnichiwa / koh-nee-chee-wah)

Person B: Hello. (konnichiwa / koh-nee-chee-wah)

Person A: My name is [Your Name]. (watashi no namae wa [Your Name] desu)

Person B: Nice to meet you. (hajimemashite / hah-jee-meh-mah-shee-teh)

Dialogue 2: Asking for Directions

Person A: Excuse me, where is the train station? (sumimasen, eki wa doko desu ka? / soo-mee-mah-sen, eh-kee wah doh-koh dess kah?)

Person B: It's over there. (asoko desu / ah-soh-koh dess)

Or: Migi (right) / hidari (left)

Dialogue 3: Ordering Food

Person A: I'm hungry. (onaka ga sukimashita / oh-nah-kah gah soo-kee-mah-shee-tah)

Person B: What would you like to eat? (nani o tabemasu ka? / nah-nee oh tah-beh-mahs kah?)

Person A: Sushi, please. (sushi wo, onegaishimasu / soo-shee-woh, oh-neh-gai-shee-mahs)

Dialogue 4: Shopping

Person A: How much is this? (kore wa ikura desu ka? / koh-ray wah ee-koo-rah dess kah?)

Person B: It's 500 yen. (gohyaku en desu / goh-hyah-koo en dess)

Dialogue 5: Emergency

Person A: Help! (tasukete! / tah-soo-keh-teh)

Person B: What happened? (doushita no? / doh-oo-shee-tah no?)

Dialogue 6: Business Meeting

Person A: I have a reservation. (yoyaku ga arimasu / yoh-yah-koo gah ah-ree-mahs)

Person B: Please have a seat. (douzo suwatte kudasai / doh-zoh su-wah-tteh koo-dah-sai)

Dialogue 7: General Conversation

Person A: Do you speak English? (eigo o hanasemasu ka? / ay-goh oh hah-nah-seh-mahs kah?)

Person B: A little. (sukoshi / su-koh-shee)

12. A Guide to the Main Cities in Japan

Heading to Japan soon? Great choice! Japan's cities are as diverse as they are fascinating, each offering its own unique flavors, sights, and experiences. Knowing a bit about what makes each city special can really level up your trip. Here's why:

- Cultural Context: Every city in Japan has its own vibe. What's cool in Tokyo might be out of place in Okinawa. A little understanding of these differences can go a long way in making your trip more respectful and fun.
- Tourist Attractions: From Tokyo's tech wonders to Kyoto's ancient temples, each city offers its own must-see spots. Knowing what you can find and where will help you pick what cities align with your interests—be it history, food, gadgets, or nature.

- Strategic Planning: Time is of the essence, especially when you're traveling. Knowing what each city is known for helps you decide where you'll get the most bang for your buck—or yen, in this case!

In the pages that follow, we'll zoom into some of Japan's standout cities like Tokyo, Kyoto, and Osaka, Nara, Hiroshima, Sapporo and Okinawa. We'll give you the lowdown on what makes each place tick so you can make the most out of your trip.

Tokyo: The Capital and Beyond

General Information

Welcome to Tokyo, Japan's bustling capital! A city where the old meets the new, Tokyo is a labyrinth of neon-lit streets and tranquil temples, state-of-the-art technology and ancient traditions. With over 13 million people, it's one of the world's most populous cities and offers something for everyone.

Why Tokyo is Important

Tokyo isn't just another big city; it's the heart of Japan in many ways—culturally, economically, and politically. As the nation's capital, it's the hub of business and government, but it's also a trendsetter in fashion, technology, and pop culture. Simply put, what happens in Tokyo doesn't just stay in Tokyo—it often influences the rest of the country and, sometimes, the world.

Language Specifics & Local Phrases

While standard Japanese is what you'll hear most often, Tokyo has its own dialect and slang, known as "Tokyo-ben." A few phrases unique to Tokyo might come in handy:

Yoroshiku ("Yoh-roh-shi-koo"): A multi-purpose phrase you can use when meeting someone, asking for a favor, or sealing a deal.

Majide ("Mah-jee-deh"): The Tokyo way of saying "Really?" or "Seriously?"

Note: People in Tokyo are generally good at understanding English compared to other parts of Japan, but a few local phrases can go a long way in breaking the ice.

Key Tourist Attractions

Tokyo is packed with things to see and do, making it impossible to experience it all in one go. But if you're short on time, here are some must-see spots:

- Shibuya Crossing: One of the busiest pedestrian crossings in the world, it's a sight to behold and a classic Tokyo experience.
- Asakusa & Senso-ji Temple: A taste of old Tokyo, this area is great for traditional crafts, foods, and the ancient Senso-ji temple.
- Tokyo Tower: For stunning views of the city, head up this iconic tower. It's like Japan's Eiffel Tower!
- Akihabara: The go-to place for electronics and anime. A paradise if you're into geek culture.
- Tsukiji Outer Market: Even though the inner wholesale market has moved to Toyosu, the outer market remains a fantastic place to enjoy fresh seafood.

Kyoto: The Heart of Traditional Japan

General Information

Say hello to Kyoto, the city that embodies the soul of traditional Japan. Known for its classical Buddhist temples, stunning gardens, imperial palaces, and traditional wooden houses, Kyoto is the place to immerse yourself in Japanese history and culture. It was Japan's capital for over one thousand years, and that deep history is felt at every turn.

Why Kyoto is Important

If Tokyo is Japan's heart, then Kyoto is its soul. This ancient city is the keeper of traditional Japanese culture, arts, and crafts. From tea ceremonies to calligraphy, from Geisha culture to Zen Buddhism, Kyoto is the epicenter of what many people consider to be "authentically Japanese." It's a living museum, and a trip here offers a deep dive into aspects of Japanese culture that have been preserved for centuries.

Language Specifics & Local Phrases

Kyoto has its own dialect known as "Kyo-kotoba" or "Kyoto-ben." While it's similar to standard Japanese, there are some unique phrases and a softer intonation. Here are a couple of local phrases to keep in mind:

Okoshiyasu ("Oh-koh-shee-yah-soo"): The Kyoto way of saying "welcome."

Dokokano? ("Doh-koh-kah-noh"): A casual way to ask "where are you going?"

Note: People in Kyoto appreciate it when you make an effort to use polite language, as the city has a more formal and traditional atmosphere compared to Tokyo.

Key Tourist Attractions

Kyoto is a city of attractions, with more temples and shrines than you could possibly visit in a single trip. However, here are some spots you shouldn't miss:

- Fushimi Inari Shrine: Famous for its thousands of vermilion torii gates that lead you up Mount Inari.
- Kinkaku-ji (The Golden Pavilion): This Zen Buddhist temple is covered in stunning gold leaf and set beside a beautiful reflective pond.
- Gion District: This is the area to see Geishas and Maikos (apprentice Geishas) and experience the age-old arts of their unique forms of entertainment.

- Arashiyama Bamboo Grove: A forest of bamboo that's unlike anything you've seen before, offering a serene walking experience.
- Nijo Castle: Known for its "nightingale floors" that chirp when walked upon, this castle offers a glimpse into the lifestyle of Japanese shoguns (the highest-ranking samurai or general).

Osaka: The Kitchen of Japan

General Information

Welcome to Osaka, a city that loves to eat and knows how to have a good time! Known as "The Kitchen of Japan," this vibrant city is a gastronomic paradise offering some of the best street foods and culinary experiences in the country. But it's not just about the food; Osaka also has a lively arts scene, bustling markets, and some of Japan's most outgoing people.

Why Osaka is Important

Osaka is Japan's third-largest city and a significant commercial hub. But its importance goes beyond the numbers. Historically, it was a merchant city, and that spirit of commerce and openness remains today. It's a place where modern life and traditions coexist, and it has its own distinct culture, dialect, and spirit that sets it apart from Tokyo and Kyoto.

Key Tourist Attractions

Osaka is brimming with activities and sights to see. Here are some must-visit attractions:

- Dotonbori: The heart of Osaka's nightlife and street food scene. Don't forget to try takoyaki (octopus balls) and okonomiyaki (savory pancake) here.
- Osaka Castle: This iconic castle offers panoramic views of the city and has a museum showcasing Osaka's history.
- Shinsaibashi: A shopper's paradise, this bustling area has everything from high-end boutiques to local shops.
- Kuromon Ichiba Market: The go-to spot for fresh produce, street food, and all kinds of Japanese goodies.
- Universal Studios Japan: One of Asia's top theme parks, it's a hit among both kids and adults.

Hiroshima: A City of Peace and Recovery

General Information

Hiroshima is a city that has become synonymous with both the devastation of war and the enduring human spirit of resilience and peace. Severely destroyed by an atomic bomb in 1945, Hiroshima has rebuilt itself as a City of Peace, advocating for the abolition of nuclear weapons and promoting a message of hope and renewal.

Why Hiroshima is Important

Hiroshima is a testament to the resilience and indomitable spirit of humankind. It stands as a poignant reminder of the consequences of war, serving as an advocate for peace and disarmament. Visiting Hiroshima is not just a historical journey but also an educational and emotional one, offering lessons in how compassion and reconciliation can triumph over destruction and despair.

Key Tourist Attractions

Here are some must-see attractions that offer both historical context and a glimpse into the city's ongoing mission of peace:

- Hiroshima Peace Memorial Park: This park is home to several monuments, including the iconic A-Bomb Dome, which survived the 1945 explosion. It's a place for reflection and education.
- Hiroshima Peace Memorial Museum: Adjacent to the park, this museum provides a haunting yet important look at the events and aftermath of the atomic bombing.
- Itsukushima Shrine: Located on nearby Miyajima Island, this Shinto shrine is famous for its "floating" torii gate and is considered one of Japan's scenic wonders.
- Hiroshima Castle: Also known as the Carp Castle, it offers a panoramic view of the city and provides a glimpse into Hiroshima's pre-war history.
- Okonomi-mura: This is a food theme park dedicated to Hiroshima-style okonomiyaki, a savory pancake filled with various ingredients. A must-visit for food lovers.

Sapporo: The Northern Frontier

General Information

Sapporo is the gateway to Japan's northernmost main island, Hokkaido. As Japan's fifth-largest city, Sapporo offers an appealing mix of urban and natural attractions. Known for its ski resorts, hot springs, and beautiful parks, it's a city that provides a stark contrast to the hustle and bustle of Tokyo.

Why Sapporo is Important

Sapporo holds a unique place in Japan as a hub of cultural diversity, natural beauty, and economic activity in Hokkaido. With its rich agricultural lands, it is a significant center for food production. Additionally, Sapporo has been the host of major international events like the 1972 Winter Olympics, making it a sports destination, particularly for winter activities. The city serves as a starting point for exploring the natural wonders of Hokkaido, from its hot springs to its expansive national parks.

Key Tourist Attractions

Here are some of the must-visit spots if you find yourself in Sapporo:

- Odori Park: The central park of Sapporo, dividing the city into north and south. It's a great spot for leisurely walks and is the site of various events, including the Sapporo Snow Festival.
- Sapporo Beer Museum: Learn about Japan's beer history and enjoy some freshly brewed Sapporo beer.
- Historic Village of Hokkaido: An open-air museum that displays various buildings from the Meiji and Taisho periods, providing a glimpse into the history of pioneer life in Hokkaido.
- Moerenuma Park: A unique park designed by Isamu Noguchi, featuring various art installations, ponds, and hills.
- Mount Moiwa: Accessible by cable car, the mountain offers one of the best panoramic views of Sapporo, especially beautiful at night.

Okinawa: The Tropical Paradise

General Information

Okinawa is an island paradise located to the south of mainland Japan. Known for its unique culture, subtropical climate, and stunning beaches, Okinawa is a world apart from the hustle and bustle of Japan's urban centers. The island is famed for its coral reefs, marine biodiversity, and a laid-back lifestyle that contributes to one of the world's highest life expectancies.

Why Okinawa is Important

Okinawa holds a special place in Japanese culture and history. It was once the center of the Ryukyu Kingdom, which had its own distinct language, culture, and traditions. Today, Okinawa is a strategically important location both for its tourism industry and its U.S. military bases. Furthermore, the Okinawan concept of "Ikigai," or a "reason for being," has intrigued researchers and wellness advocates around the world.

Language Specifics & Local Phrases

Okinawa has its own native language, Okinawan, although standard Japanese is widely spoken and understood. However, knowing a few local words or phrases can enrich your experience:

Haisai ("Hi-sigh"): A general greeting, equivalent to "hello," used by both men and women.

Mensore ("Men-soh-ray"): An Okinawan word for "welcome."

Note: Okinawans are known for their hospitality and openness. A simple greeting in the local language can go a long way in making connections.

Key Tourist Attractions

Okinawa offers a blend of natural beauty and historical sites. Here are some key attractions you shouldn't miss:

- Shuri Castle: Once the palace of the Ryukyu Kingdom, this UNESCO World Heritage Site is a must-visit for history buffs.
- Katsuren Castle Ruins: Another UNESCO World Heritage Site, offering stunning panoramic views of the ocean.
- Okinawa Churaumi Aquarium: One of the world's largest aquariums, it's famous for its massive Kuroshio Tank.
- Naha's Kokusai Street: The main street in Okinawa's capital, Naha, filled with shops, restaurants, and bars. A perfect place to try Okinawan cuisine and buy souvenirs.

- Beaches and Water Sports: Okinawa is surrounded by coral reefs, making it an ideal location for snorkeling, scuba diving, and other water activities. Katsuren Peninsula and the Kerama Islands are particularly popular spots.

Nara: The Cradle of Japanese Tradition

General Information

Nara is a city steeped in history and tradition, located in the Kansai region of Japan, not far from Osaka and Kyoto. Famous for its well-preserved temples, beautiful parks, and free-roaming deer, Nara was Japan's first permanent capital and remains a repository of cultural heritage. With its tranquil atmosphere and scenic beauty, Nara serves as a serene escape from the urban hustle.

Why Okinawa is Important

Nara holds a distinguished place in the history of Japan. It was the capital during the Nara period (710–794 AD), a time when many of Japan's most significant cultural developments, including the spread of Buddhism, took root. Nara is home to several UNESCO World Heritage Sites and offers an invaluable look into early Japanese art, architecture, and religion.

Key Tourist Attractions

Nara offers a range of cultural and natural attractions that invite contemplation and wonder:

- Todai-ji Temple: Home to the Great Buddha statue, this temple is a must-visit site and a UNESCO World Heritage landmark.
- Nara Park: Famous for its friendly, free-roaming deer, which are considered messengers of the gods.
- Kasuga Taisha Shrine: Known for its beautiful lantern-lined paths, this Shinto shrine is another UNESCO World Heritage Site.
- Naramachi: A well-preserved area showcasing traditional Japanese architecture and artisan shops.
- Isuien Garden: A beautifully landscaped Japanese garden, perfect for a peaceful stroll.
- Horyu-ji Temple: One of the world's oldest wooden structures, offering a glimpse into ancient Buddhist architecture.

Nara offers an enriching travel experience steeped in tradition and natural beauty, making it a destination that can deepen your understanding of Japan's past and its enduring cultural values.

13. Bonus: Itinerary

7-Day Itinerary

Day 1: Arrival in Tokyo

• Morning: Arrival and hotel check-in

• Afternoon: Asakusa and Senso-ji Temple

• Evening: Shinjuku for dinner and nightlife

Day 2: Tokyo Exploration

• Morning: Tsukiji Fish Market

• Afternoon: Imperial Palace Gardens

• Evening: Shibuya Crossing and dinner

Day 3: Travel to Kyoto

- Morning: Shinkansen (fast train) to Kyoto

- Afternoon: Kinkaku-ji (The Golden Pavilion)

- Evening: Stroll along the Gion District

Day 4: Kyoto Exploration

- Morning: Fushimi Inari Shrine

- Afternoon: Arashiyama Bamboo Grove

- Evening: Traditional Tea Ceremony

Day 5: Travel to Osaka

- Morning: Shinkansen to Osaka

- Afternoon: Osaka Castle

- Evening: Dotonbori Food Street

Day 6: Day Trip to Hiroshima

- Morning: Shinkansen to Hiroshima

- Day: Peace Memorial Park and Hiroshima Castle

- Evening: Return to Osaka

Day 7: Departure from Osaka or Return to Tokyo

- Morning: Last-minute souvenir shopping

- Afternoon: Head to the airport for departure or return to Tokyo if you're flying out from there

14-Day Itinerary

Day 1: Arrival in Tokyo

- Morning: Arrival and hotel check-in

- Afternoon: Visit Asakusa and Senso-ji Temple

- Evening: Dinner at a local Izakaya (restaurant)

Day 2: Tokyo Exploration

- Tokyo Tower

- Meiji Shrine

- Shibuya Crossing

Day 3: Day Trip to Nikko

- Toshogu Shrine

- Lake Chuzenji

Day 4: Travel to Kyoto

- Morning: Shinkansen (fast train) to Kyoto

- Afternoon: Kinkaku-ji (Golden Pavilion)

Day 5-6: Kyoto Exploration

- Fushimi Inari Shrine

- Arashiyama Bamboo Grove

- Gion District

Day 7: Travel to Osaka

- Osaka Castle

- Dotonbori

Day 8: Day Trip to Nara

- Nara Park

- Todai-ji Temple

Day 9: Travel to Hiroshima

- Peace Memorial Park

- Hiroshima Castle

Day 10: Day Trip to Miyajima Island

- Itsukushima Shrine

- Mount Misen

Day 11: Travel to Sapporo

- Evening: Explore Sapporo Beer Museum

Day 12: Sapporo Exploration

- Odori Park

- Mount Moiwa

Day 13: Travel Back to Tokyo

- Last-minute shopping in Akihabara or Harajuku

- Farewell dinner

Day 14: Departure

14. Conclusion

Your journey through Japan isn't just a tour of places; it's a deep dive into a kaleidoscope of cultures, histories, and social norms that make each city stand out. From the technological wonders of Tokyo to the ancient traditions in Kyoto, the food haven in Osaka to the winter paradise of Sapporo, each city offers a unique facet of Japan's multifaceted identity. Understanding what makes each city special not only enriches your overall experience but helps you make the most out of every moment spent in the Land of the Rising Sun.

Arigatou Gozaimasu!

Could you kindly spare a moment to share your thoughts on the book by leaving a review? Your gesture would be immensely valued and deeply appreciated!

Journal Pages

Be sure to pack this book on your journey to Japan! Utilize these lined pages to jot down new phrases you pick up along the way. This space is also perfect for chronicling your adventures—where you've been, the sights you've seen, the foods you've tasted, and the unforgettable moments you experience!

Printed in Great Britain
by Amazon

37148180R00056